About this Book

An Intimate, Personal, Inspiring, and Encouraging Journey of Raising Taylor
By Sharon Taylor-Harris
Her Loving Mom

As a little girl, I always admired the strong women in my life: my mom, grandmother, and aunt. They all worked and raised their families. At some point in their lives, they each became single moms. Because of work, they balanced family life as best they could to support their children in the home along with academics, events, and activities. I always knew that when I started my family, I had to put more work into being an original mom. I knew that I had to raise my daughter in and outside the home while giving her academic support. I was thrilled to become a mother and excited with every challenge that came my way.

Raising Taylor takes you through a mother and daughter's personal journey. We moved from various school districts in order to find the right fit. We overcame challenges. We believe that everything we gave up will return to us in time with great faith. After working hard to achieve her best, Taylor finally found her hero, Superwoman, and sets an example for all other children who look to follow in her academic footsteps.

About the Author

Sharon Taylor-Harris is a first-time book writer and the author of *Raising Taylor, Finding Superwoman Our Way*. She worked in a demanding position for many years while raising Taylor. She has shown strength, guidance, and courage of leadership as head of the household as a single mom. She now lives in Florida with her daughter Taylor and still supports Taylor in her college years. She gives Taylor the space she needs to make her own decisions. Her mom is still standing by to help her in any way she needs.

Instagram: @sharon.taylorharris

For general questions or comments, please email Sharon Taylor-Harris: staylorhred@yahoo.com

Raising Taylor
Finding Superwoman

Raising Taylor Finding Superwoman
THE DIFFICULT CHOICES MANY PARENTS FIND HARD TO MAKE

Sharon Taylor-Harris

Copyright © 2021 Sharon Taylor-Harris

All rights reserved. No part of this book may be reproduced or transmitted in any form or by any means, electronic or mechanical, including photocopying, recording, or by any information storage and retrieval system, except in the case of brief quotations embodied in critical articles and reviews, without prior written permission of the publisher.

ISBN Paperback: 978-0-578-87552-1
ISBN Hardcover: 978-1-7368926-0-2
ISBN eBook: 978-1-7368926-1-9

Printed in the United States of America

Interior Design: Creative Publishing Book Design

*I dedicate my last page to Randy Pausch.
He was a professor and Imagineer for Walt Disney.
His book* The Last Lecture, *has shown people how dreams
do come true and how to imagine yourself
doing the things you always dreamed of.
Thank you, Randy, for giving people an
imaginary look into their own world.*

---

*To my daughter with love:
Taylor, who inspired me to write about her journey
and to follow my passion by being the best mom I could be.*

Table of Content

Introduction. 1
First Grade, Elementary School 5
Second Grade, Elementary School. 11
Third Grade, Elementary School 13
Fourth Grade, Elementary School. 15
Fifth Grade, Elementary School 23
Sixth Grade, Middle School 35
Seventh Grade, Middle School 41
Eighth Grad, Middle School 43
Ninth Grade, High School 57
Tenth Grade, High School 61
Eleventh Grade, High School 75
Twelfth Grade, High School. 85
Conclusion 99
Taylor's Update 103

Introduction

Waking up, lying in bed looking at the ceiling, I thought, *Wow my daughter starts elementary school today.* Her first years of growing had passed me by. Was she prepared for her first year of school? Had I missed anything? Was I prepared for her to go alone? These were the questions I had to ponder before heading out the door. Just as any first-time parent would have done, I arranged time off from work that morning just to walk hand and hand with her through the school's doors and kiss her goodbye. I stood behind the classroom door to watch her interact with the other kids and to see how she responded to them. Being an only child, Taylor loved to interact with children. She wanted to learn how to share and bond in a special way. School was a great place for her to learn and grow. She handled her first day of school like she had been going for years. She was quiet and enjoyed the other students, but she also responded to her teacher if asked to. Once I was confident she was going to be okay, I felt comfortable leaving the school. Teachers stood in the hall and watched me. I could imagine them thinking and whispering, "This fruitcake! Go home, lady, or go to work. Your daughter is in a new world. Now let her enjoy it," as they laughed quietly. I politely presented a fake smile to them and headed to the exit doors. I felt good when I arrived at work and soon felt my daughter was comfortable in her new world. Although my day was long, I was excited to return to my daughter and ask her about her first day of school.

I worked as a contract employee with YOH Aviation on-site at the Boeing Company in St. Louis, Missouri. I specialized in preparing reports for two different programs, C-17 Cargo Transporter Aircrafts and the F/18 Fighter Jets Program. My work was detailed and required a lot of attention. I needed to focus without worrying about home and family life. My workdays were filled with me running out after work to after-school daycare. With my kid hand in one hand and my purse and laptop in the other, I would leave after-school daycare minutes before closing. My workday never ended. After spending time with Taylor in the evening and asking how her day was, I would cook dinner for us. Then we enjoyed laughing around the table. Bath time and playtime before bed were a must before she drifted off into la-la land. When she fell asleep, I returned to work from our home office. I would open my laptop and finish any projects that I left unfinished because I had to run out to pick up Taylor.

I loved my work just as much as I loved being a mom. I was happy in my own skin and with my accomplishments in the aerospace industry. I was also happy to see Taylor so joyfully attending school. I was young, strong, and had lots of energy. I loved being on-the-go. It made me think fast and kept my mind active and sharp.

Very soon after having Taylor, Taylor's dad and I separated. I became Taylor's only parent in the home. I was Taylor's mother, father, sister, brother, provider, comforter, safety net, and decision maker. It was my first, second, and third job. It wasn't easy to accomplish, but I tried my best to balance my fears of failing. I would wake at 5:30am and prepare for the day. Taylor would wake at 6:00am and prepare for her day alongside me. We would start out by traveling to before-and after-school daycare around 6:45am. I arrived at work no later than 7:30am for a fresh morning start. That was when I found my happiest times. Taylor was in a safe environment at school, and I was passionate about my job. I found a love for aerospace in the business industry. I went from working with an engineer fastener company to aerospace in a matter of years.

Aerospace gave me the challenge to learn something new. I worked hard to showcase my skills and to provide quality work on each project I completed. While working as a contract employee on-site at the Boeing Company, I learned how ethics and principles can be applied to one's everyday life. Ethics training was mandatory at the Boeing Company. I learned how to do the right thing and make the right choices for the company, clients, and the projects I was working on. I take these ethics and principles with me wherever I go and apply them to all areas of my life. My job was my escape as a single mom. I released my stress and worries about Taylor and our life at home into projects that made me feel knowledgeable and experienced. I will tell you that I did worry about how our life would turn out, but I grew stronger in faith as each year flew by. I worked as hard as I could to provide the best while raising Taylor no matter how much of me it took. It took a lot of me and my own personal time.

SO HERE'S MY STORY.

First Grade
Elementary School

Overjoyed and excited, Taylor has started her first day of school. She made new friends, wrote, and completed worksheets during class. She ate lunch with other students as a group and, of course, loved recess. How could she ever forget recess? With a playground to challenge her physical skills, she had all she needed. After we had talked about her day, I knew Taylor's learning had begun and her academic journey was headed in the right direction. Taylor was doing solid work. She was engaging with classroom activities. She had even learned a system when arriving home: She would have a snack first, do her homework, and then have dinner, bathe, and finally play if time permitted. Taylor looked forward to each school-day morning because she knew she would see other kids and learn how to grow with her class as a group. Each day, she woke up with the same joy and excitement. She just could not seem to get enough of being a first-time student in school.

Soon after school started, I remember watching the news and growing worried. Our newscast stated that the Riverview Garden School District was having trouble keeping their accreditation. I held on to hope that things would change over the year, but something gave me an ill feeling about the district in which my daughter was enrolled.

As the year went by, Taylor and I enjoyed her first year of school, approaching it with excitement, and we tried to put the school district troubles behind us. She never forgot the feeling of belonging to a group and making her first friends. But I grew sad and disappointed with new updates that my daughter's school district was about to lose their accreditation. This disappointment was a tough pill to swallow. I just could not imagine my daughter attending an unaccredited school and not being prepared for her college years. I wanted more for my daughter's education so that she could experience great things that I did not receive. I grew more and more stressed because someday that joy of going to school would eventually disappear in my daughter's eyes, and I knew exactly why.

I was committed to staying in the community we both loved and searched for a school in the area that produced high academic scores. I researched material at work during lunch and afterwork just to give me hope that a school with great academics in my community would accept my daughter. I was excited that I found one school to pursue. I traveled to the school with high hopes and spoke to the principal about my concerns that the school Taylor was attending was not meeting their academic standards. I told the principal I wanted my daughter to be engaged with a group of students who were as bright and passionate as she was. I took my daughter's school records to show her academic test scores. Griffin Elementary was the school Taylor and I had decided to pursue. The principal was impressed that I had done my homework and research on both schools. But in the end, the principal at the alternative school Griffin Elementary would not accept my daughter as a transfer. To this day, I'm still not sure of why, even though I lived in the district and offered to transport my daughter to and from school at my own expense. I was just told that the transfer could not happen.

Because of this, I was terribly distraught. My daughter was doing well in school but the overall academics at her current elementary school were not good. Keeping my daughter at Danforth Elementary school meant that she would carry some burden of representing this school with good grades and good assessment test scores to show that the school did have some students who performed well. But in the end, I wondered if this school, as settle as she was, was the best place for my daughter. It did not have the teaching required to move her forward and challenge her skills. Teachers were too busy trying to help other students catch on and catch up with their classroom material. With teachers leaving my daughter to work on her own while they worked with students who were slow to learn, my daughter felt isolated in a very small group. This group worked alone on projects they already knew how to do until a decision was made to move forward in learning together as a group.

On July 1, 2007, it was official. Riverview Gardens School District had lost its accreditation. Having my daughter graduate from a school district with accreditation meant so much more to me than keeping her in a place where she felt comfortable. I wanted her to be proud she contributed to a class that has worked equally as hard to receive the best academic education they possibly could. She deserved to show great pride in a school with great teachers, great students, and a great accreditation. That hope I felt for Taylor ended when Riverview Gardens School District lost their accreditation, and I knew now I needed to do something. *What* was the question.

What Must I Do Now?

Second grade was about to start, and I had little time to come up with a plan. I pondered sending Taylor to private school, which I truly could not afford being a single mom with so many other bills to pay. I also considered staying in the Riverview Garden School District. I prayed that they would regain their accreditation soon, although I had little hope that would happen. Then I pondered the option of us moving to a new school district that was accredited with good academics and good overall state testing scores. I chose this last choice. My daughter and I decided it was time to move on and say goodbye to our community and for her to be enrolled in a school district that was accredited and could challenge her skills. This choice is one many parents struggle to make. I had to make this decision as a single mom. Taylor's dad was long gone by then. But in the end, for my daughter, I knew I had to make this choice so she could have a good chance of receiving a great education from an accredited school that would prepare her for her college years.

HERE COMES THE BOOM

Second Grade Elementary School

Taylor's second grade was just exciting as the beginning of her first. She was ready Freddy. *So, let's bring it on!* Arrowpoint Elementary School was the new school in the new district we moved to. New school, new teachers, and new friends. *Way to go, Taylor! You're off to a great start*, I told her. Taylor second grade was a walk in the park. That excitement and joy came back into her eyes. She looked forward to waking up and dressing for school with lunch box and backpack in tow. *Wow!* We made a great decision moving to a new community. However, we both were sad that we left our friends, neighbors, home, and the community we loved so much. We knew that we had to give something up in order to gain something else. We gave up a house with a nice-size backyard and patio with a driveway and garage of our own to live in a small two-bedroom townhouse with neighbors just steps away with shared outside parking.

We were disappointed, but knew it was all for a community that had an accredited school.

Heading off to school in the mornings, Taylor's days were long because she attended before-and-after-school care so I could work. This was a challenge I had to overcome. Being a single mom, I had very little family help with Taylor. So I depended on outside help along with the YMCA Center to fill the gaps and provide Taylor with a safe environment. Balancing work, daycare, and Taylor's school were all added to my busy schedule while working in aerospace. But that didn't matter. Taylor was on a roll. Her daily routine was working well. Her class was all on the same academic page, same level, same pace, moving in the right direction at the same time with classroom pride.

On Taylor's second grade year-end report card, her teacher had written, *Taylor is a real pleasure to have in class. She's eager to learn. Well spoken. She's a competitive student who takes pride in her work. She looks forward to the next task at hand. What a joy to have her in class.* That praise was what every parent wanted to hear and see about their child at the end of the school year. This affirmation took some of the pain away, even if we could not replace our home, our friends, our good neighbors, and our old community that had meant so much to us over the years. I was proud that I had made a difficult decision by moving to a new community. It turned into a good choice for my daughter's education. We had to move on!

BREEZING THROUGH
Third Grade Elementary School

Holding her head high with her pencils and notebook in hand, Taylor walked the halls of third grade like a champ. She knew the system. Taylor thought to herself, *Yes! Who is it? It's me; I've been here before,* giggling to herself. She looked forward to her new school year. Taylor slid into her classroom and released a little sigh. If you can't tell, for the third year in a row, I was still walking my daughter to class on the first day…laughing. Looking behind the partial glass door, I saw that she looked comfortable. She was smiling, and that was a good thing. She was happy to be a part of a classroom in an accredited school district. Taylor breezed through her third grade with a big smile on her face, and part of a growing group of students. Not much to say about third grade, but she did well in her academics and then moved on to fourth grade.

TAYLOR SEEMS DIFFERENT

Fourth Grade Elementary School

Fourth grade arrived. Taylor was ready to start the school year, but something happened during her fourth-grade year that threw me for a loop. Sure of herself, Taylor started off the year as a proficient student. Her grades were good, steady, and consistent. I wouldn't say she worked any harder that year than any other. She just did the work as it was presented and made sure it was turned in on time. But I could tell Taylor needed to add something extra to her schedule.

Over dinner we both talked about what could be added. She expressed her passion to learn how to play a music instrument. The violin was her choice. A big smile appeared across my face. So, I said, "Well, then let's do it." She exclaimed, "Yeah!" I was happy for her enthusiasm, even if I knew this new activity would come with its own set of challenges.

We were able to enroll her in the music class at school on time, though finding a violin for Taylor was challenging. I traveled in and outside the area to find a violin to rent. No luck in sight. I called every music store in the surrounding area, and they told me the same thing. Most parents reserve them at the end of the school year so they can have one available for the upcoming school year. At the last music store, I traveled to, the music store owner presented me with a beautiful brand-new violin to purchase. I could not afford to pay the price for it though, so I needed a used or rented one to work with my budget. Before leaving the music store with a sad look on my face, the owner offered a used flute to rent instead. I said it would do, and it was better to have an alternate than to have no instrument at all. "I'll take it." I said with a half-smile. Before I turned to leave, the music store owner told me that if for some reason a used violin was returned, he would put me first on the waiting list to rent it. The charge would be the same, and he would deliver it to the school where we could exchange the flute for the violin. That would work, and I was happy to accept the offer. I then presented the flute to Taylor and explained that the music store had loaned out all violins for the school year. She was not totally disappointed. She just wanted to try something new and said the flute would do for now. I promised Taylor at the end of the year I would reserve the violin for the upcoming school year so that she would have her choice of a music instrument to play in class.

Surprise

Before the first week of school had ended, the music store contacted me and stated they would be delivering a

The Difficult Choices Many Parents Find Hard to Make

violin to my daughter's school. This was great news and more convenient for me not to travel the long miles back to the music store. The music store made a routine trip to the school monthly to repair and tune instruments for students and the exchange happened right before their first visit. Someone had returned a used violin and sure enough, the owner remembered that I wanted to exchange the flute for my daughter's first choice. I didn't tell Taylor about the exchange. I let her music teacher give her the exciting news in class. Taylor was totally surprised. She accepted her violin in front of the whole orchestra class with joy and was able to join in with the other violinists.

When Taylor arrived home from school, she gave me her exciting news with a great big hug. So now Taylor had occupied her mind with something new. She was learning a new skill. The violin also gave Taylor something I could not: freedom of expression. Taylor was able to express herself while playing the violin. When she felt sad, she would pick up her musical instrument and play until she felt better. When she felt great, she would play with lots of joy. Learning to play the violin was a great outlet for Taylor, and she learned to play with grace throughout her school years.

Toward the end of the school year, the school put together a music presentation. All music students were able to showcase their talents. Sitting in a pearl-white blouse and black pants, Taylor was in the front row of her orchestra class. Nervous but excited, she played her violin with grace and harmony. I invited her family to take part in her joy, and they stayed to the end to congratulate Taylor on a job well done. *Click, click, click.* All cameras were busy snapping photos of Taylor with her violin. I was so proud of my daughter. I just could not get enough of the joy and smile on her face. We found what was missing, or so I thought.

As the year went by, she completed her academic work well. She played the violin gracefully, and teachers were pleased to have her as part of the group. But after fourth grade ended, Taylor dropped another bomb on me. She said that she had outgrown the school. I said, "WHAT! Repeat that?" Laughing! I was shocked. I truly thought I had found the school district to which Taylor would contribute to in the coming years. I asked Taylor what was it that she needed. She said that she needed to be challenged more.

Oh! Okay! I thought, *My goodness what a kid.*

I thought, I have enough on my plate with balancing a challenging career in aerospace and making sure my daughter was in a safe school environment. But this new challenge of Taylor's was unexpected.

I told Taylor that we could look into finding her what she needed more of. But I was sure she was already challenged by trying to keep up with her music and her academics at the same time. I was certain she had enough to work with. Then she said she wanted to learn new and different things. I knew the school had a good academic list of courses, but Taylor expressed that she wanted to learn a foreign language which her current elementary school did not offer at the time. I could not argue with her, and that was one area her elementary school had not offered students during the year of 2011. So, I began another journey to change the school district I thought was a perfect fit.

Here We Go Again, Packing And Saying Goodbye

This time I wanted to be sure that the school Taylor attended had a wider range of class options with a continuous improvement plan to grow their curriculum by offering several different electives like sewing, cooking, and dance, along with foreign languages. I didn't look for the best school district, just one that was accredited and on the right track. I knew with a great plan in place, they would continue to improve, and Taylor would reach her goals. After my search, I chose the Parkway School District. It was required that all students take a foreign language of their choice: French, German, or Spanish before senior graduation. That was a plus. They wanted all students to have access to learn a new tool and to use it regularly.

Parkway School District also had a communication plan in place for parents, teachers, and students. Parents had to sign off on various paperwork that students brought home to let the school district know they received the information, read it, and understood it. Parents were also the point of contact for growing concerns with their students. If grades were questionable or homework was missing, teachers and counselors could reach out to parents, along with students, for clarity. If any issues arose that were too overwhelming for students to handle on their own, parents had to state their child's next move to ensure their child would stay on course. I loved how Parkway's teachers communicated with the students first but also followed up with the parents for a plan to ensure students were on the right track. It made me feel secure that in case my daughter happened to forget to fill me in on issues with a difficult course or that she was too ashamed to tell me she was having problems; I could be sure that her teachers would follow up with me. What a great system! I would also like to note that the Parkway School District had great attendance percentage, which was growing each year with more students having access to academic learning in the school. This was important to me, because the school district and I knew if the students were not in school, teachers could not teach them. Students had to attend school on a regular basis, so that in-classroom teaching could be performed, and in-classroom questions could be answered. Their plan was to make sure no student was left behind or left out.

Parkway School District's academics average was above the state's average to hold an accreditation, but the district was not satisfied. They knew they could do better in time, and with a continuous improvement plan their numbers would increase in academics, attendance, and overall graduation percentage. This striving is what excited me about the Parkway School District. Although there were better school districts in the area with higher academic numbers, I knew the Parkway

School District had the level of learning Taylor needed with a continuous improvement plan that would motivate, inspire, encourage and give her insight that she could achieve her highest goals. So we invested in the Parkway School District as they invested in my daughter's education.

Fifth Grade Elementary School

Fifth grade has started, and Taylor was finding her way. Not just in a new school but a different county as well—West County to be exact. Taylor was treading water lightly to learn how the system worked. She was utilizing the library, studying hard, and sharing with other students. Taylor became comfortable with the Parkway School District. Review time came as the first trimester ended. Her reviews were good, and I was another pleased parent.

But Wait: Something Horrible Happened!

Taylor had never been a sick child. She had the normal colds and ear infections, but they all cleared up with medication as she grew older. A few weeks into fall 2012 at the age of ten, Taylor became ill and needed to see her pediatrician. I was told at that time that Taylor had drainage from her ears and needed medicine to clear it up. We filled the prescriptions that the pediatrician gave us and started her on the medication. A few days later, Taylor broke out with a rash, the first sign that something was terribly wrong. I took her back to the pediatrician and was told to stop all medication and start her on some new medicine. I filled this new prescription, and we started it as directed the next day.

A few days after that, Taylor slept the whole day on Sunday. She was tired and weak. By Monday morning, I asked Taylor to wash her face, so I could take her back to the doctor, and she said she could not. I noticed she also could barely walk. So, I grabbed Taylor and put her in the back seat of the car, and we rushed to the doctor's office. When I pulled up at curbside, I had to get a wheelchair for Taylor because she was unable to walk. Her motor skills were shutting down. I became frightened but needed to stay strong and show no fear so that Taylor would stay calm. As we made it to the doctor's office, I told the pediatrician about the new medication she was taking. She looked at Taylor for fewer than five minutes and instructed me to take her to the emergency room.

A nurse escorted us to the emergency room from the medical office, which was connected to the hospital. We waited our turn as I held Taylor and ensured her everything would be okay. During evaluation, Taylor was asked to stand and weigh herself. I told the nurse she could not, but I could help her if she desperately needed that information.

After the evaluation, we entered one of the examination rooms. The emergency room doctor pulled Taylor's records and then proceeded to speak to me. "Sharon is it?" they asked. I said, "Yes. What is the problem with Taylor?" I told the doctor that she had been complaining about having a cold, but her pediatrician stated that she had drainage from her ears and gave her medication to clear it up. After being allergic to the first medication, she was then given amoxicillin tablets. She also had a flu shot while she was in the office during her visit. And that was what triggered a trip to the emergency room.

The emergency room doctor stated that, "I can see Taylor has never been admitted into the hospital before," and I said, "You are correct." Taylor had ear infections and slight colds but nothing that caused her to be admitted into the hospital. The emergency room doctor at that time said, "Let's do two things. First a spinal tap to draw fluid. Then an MRI to see how much fluid she has and where exactly it is." I said, "OK," and told Taylor to be very still while they performed the spinal tap. I whispered in her ear that everything was going to be okay. Taylor replied," Okay Mom."

Fluid was drawn and tested. The results came back the next hour. "Nothing to be alarmed about," the emergency room doctor said. "Now let's do the MRI." After the MRI, I was told that there was fluid in her head, more than what should be, but a group of emergency room doctors thought that the fluid would release on its own from her body. "So, let's admit Taylor overnight and see how she is in the morning." We did so, and I spent the night waiting for this fluid to release from my daughter's head. What a horrible night that was for me! No sleeping and lots of worry.

Morning arrived and no luck. The children's floor doctor came in and evaluated Taylor. He noticed that things had not changed, so they said to give it a few more days. I was beginning to panic. Taylor had double vision, and her motor skills were lost somewhere in her body. I helped my daughter feed herself like I did when she was six months old. I was feeding her again at the age of ten, and this was not sitting well with me. There was lots of fluid in her head, and we were not sure from where it came.

More days passed, and the fluid did not release. The children's chief of staff called another neurologist over to evaluate, and review my daughter's charts, and to give me a second opinion. Ten minutes was all it took for the new neurologist to give me two options: to have surgery at the hospital where Taylor was currently admitted or move her to the hospital where he was on staff. Where a group of trained professionals could run detailed tests to try and figure out what caused all this fluid to land in Taylor's head as well as perform the necessary surgery.

Distraught and confused, I packed our things up quickly and moved to another hospital because my daughter needed surgery that night to try to figure out how this fluid got into her head. The new neurologists called a special unit to bring Taylor to his hospital by ambulance.

I explained to Taylor that she needed to have a procedure done right away. She was frightened because I could not travel

The Difficult Choices Many Parents Find Hard to Make

with her in the ambulance to the next hospital, but I comfort her by telling her that she was going to be okay and I would be there before she went into surgery. When I arrived a few minutes after Taylor, she was already admitted to an intensive care room and being prepped for surgery. Taylor was exhausted, but we needed to start this process: the road to getting her healthy again.

I froze when the authorization form for surgery was given to me to sign. I had so many unanswered questions. What will happen in surgery? Would she be okay after? What were the side effects?

Should I sign the authorization form? I wondered. I just felt lost, wondering how we got there. The cracks in the ceiling were falling, and my world was torn upside down. About to break down, I managed to sign the form and off Taylor went to surgery. There was no time to discuss details with her surgeon, so I placed my daughter into his hands and prayed for a good outcome.

My mind raced a mile a minute. Bad thoughts appeared, and I was overcome with panic attacks and heart-racing moments. I was a complete mess, standing in the middle of the floor of the children's intensive care unit. Nurses looked as I melted into a lost mom. While Taylor was in surgery, I had to tell the story of how we got there all over again to the administrator to clarify what happened to Taylor from the beginning. Her transfer papers arrived and those were helpful because all records from the first hospital were electronically sent to the new hospital with Taylor.

After giving information on Taylor's journey to surgery, I waited to see her. My ten-year-old who just had surgery on the temple of her forehead. I was told that they inserted a long tube in my daughter's head to slowly drain the fluid out. Taylor started to come around and cried. I held her hand and assured her that she was going to be just fine and that I would stay with her through her journey. The nurse said the same thing. As I prayed and watched her until day broke, the intensive care doctors arrived to evaluate Taylor after her surgery. Her face appeared to be returning to normal. Before the surgery it was still full of fluid and very plump. The tube in her head was draining fluid, and I was pleased to see the infection as it released. Taylor felt a little relief but was still weak and sad. She was unsure of what was going to happen next. Since this was a slow drain, things were not mot moving fast at all, but doctors could see improvements day by day.

Meanwhile, lots of blood was drawn for tests to see what had caused Taylor's pain and how so much fluid ended up in her head. I was told that over one hundred tests were completed, but there was no clear answer on what the cause was. The doctors were puzzled and just told me that she had an infection, and they could not pinpoint what it was or where it came from or why it landed in her head. That was the hardest part of my daughter's hospital stay.

We didn't know how to prevent it from happening again. I was not happy, not satisfied, but my hands were tied. All I could do was nurse my daughter back to health and accept not knowing what caused it.

Days went by, then weeks, and the tube was still slowly draining fluid and infection from Taylor's head. I could see my daughter's face returning to normal as each day went by. But I grew disappointed that the tube was still attached to her head.

Taylor was evaluated and now ready to try eating on her own again. We started with popsicles to see if she could suck and swallow. Then, we had a hospital test to see if she could eat solid foods like crackers and pudding. Taylor slowly grew from popsicles and pudding (which she began to like for breakfast), to solid food slowly. She was able to feed herself and keep her food down, a huge accomplishment in the moment. I was feeling better, but this tube was still inside my daughter's head and it was beginning to bother me.

We then received word that Taylor was able to move from intensive care unit to a floor unit room with other children in the hospital. This was great news to me and Taylor. Taylor just graduated to a new freer level. This level had regular hospital rooms where children could venture out and see other kids, chat, do homework, and participate in hospital events during their stay such as art and craft classes. Children on this level were not monitored as frequently as they were in the intensive care unit. Taylor was slowly feeding herself again, and I was grateful. Her doctor told me that in time things would get better, and I held onto hope.

She was unable to bathe herself and comb her hair due to lost motor skills. We worked with Taylor as though these skills had been attacked by the infection, which was exactly what happened. After we finally received word to remove the tube and drain, I was told that we had to take things slowly. She needed help to learn how to walk again. The best thing to do was to enroll Taylor in physical therapy and to send her home with a cane to help her walk and balance. Taylor did physical therapy three times a week at Children's Hospital Therapy along with home exercises. She also had to complete occupational and speech therapy. She did so in no time. Her memory was still intact and still strong. It was a blessing that those areas were not affected, or damaged, but physical therapy took a long time.

Taylor's balance became a major problem. She could not seem to balance without support. Children's physical therapy assistants worked hard to get her stable, but her progress just wasn't moving fast enough. Taylor's insurance company decided to end payments for physical therapy because they thought Taylor's progress should have been better and the prognosis should have been a higher percentage. In physical therapy, Taylor was graded on each exercise. Climbing stairs, jumping, walking in a straight line without touching the walls, and standing on one leg. Since she was struggling with physical therapy, I had to put her in homebound teaching because she just could not walk straight without bumping into people or walls even with the help of a cane. It was not good for her to

The Difficult Choices Many Parents Find Hard to Make

be in a school environment with no support, and it became too challenging for Taylor not to have her balance in school. We worked hard with home exercises, and we continued to work on her balance years later after her surgery. She was doing better, and it was a continuing process for her to improve.

Because of some swelling in her head, we found out that Taylor needed more physical therapy to work on her balance. I was very concerned that she would not improve enough to walk without a cane, so I made an appointment with the hospital balance center called the ear, nose, and throat doctor at the Advance Center for Medicine for a check-up. After Taylor's evaluation and balance test, the doctor recommend more therapy, but this time a method called vestibular therapy which concentrates on specific physical motor skills and balance. The doctor had to call Taylor's insurance company and state that more physical therapy was needed, and it would benefit her recovery. The insurance company finally agreed after a long, lengthy phone call. But this time the ear, nose, and throat doctor needed to see a weekly report on Taylor's progress. Her insurance company also wanted to be updated weekly to ensure Taylor was on the right track with her new therapy order.

Taylor's diagnosis was 386.2 Vertigo Evaluate and Treat. After many visits to physical therapy, off we went again to more physical therapy but with a new-improved order. This time we had more of a structure of what areas on which we should concentrate on. Her new therapist office worked with a small group and had late evening hours to work with Taylor. This was great news for me because I was balancing work and Taylor's physical therapy visits each week. I included Taylor's appointments in my work meeting schedule to ensure that we were present and on-time for all her visits. I was not stressed because I knew that this new physical therapy order was good for Taylor, and we could see her improvements within weeks.

The therapist concentrated on stairs since there were more than plenty available. Her office was on the second level floor. She then proceeded to work with Taylor on walking in a straight line and balancing on one leg then hopping. After weeks and a reevaluation, the doctor stated that she had improved, but he wanted her to continue therapy a little longer. We did so, and Taylor had improved enough to return to school and try out her new skills without the assistance of a cane. In the end, Taylor had Cerebellitis, hydrocephalus, a condition that lands fluid in between brain tissues. My daughter's treatment was surgery to insert a tube in her head and slowly drain as much fluid as needed to bring back normal functions and to minimize any side effects.

Returning to School

Taylor returned to finish her fifth-grade year. Her class welcomed her back with get well cards, hugs, and candy. Taylor held back tears of joy and joined in with the class. She never lost a beat because of her homebound teacher. That young lady was great for my daughter. They worked well together through the evening hours catching up on what Taylor missed while hospitalized, to prepare for her to return to school. At yearend review time, Taylor's teacher told me she was concerned that Taylor had lost a lot of organizational skills. Taylor's desk and locker became a junk pile with everything falling out. Taylor's teacher was patient and picked up after behind her, but after our conversation I got the feeling her teacher was tired of it. I told her that this was one area we would have to continue to work on because of Taylor's loss of physical and motor skills during her hospital stay, but I assured her teacher that it was a work in progress.

Taylor's year turned out great. After a hard year of catch-up work, she became a Spirt of Excellence Student. Spirt of Excellence was awarded to those students of diversity and who had received As and Bs and held an GPA of 3.5 or higher throughout the calendar year along with excellence in academics, communication, arts, and community. Students were rewarded with an evening program that consisted of a celebration with awards, entertainment, songs, speeches, and special awards given to teachers and alumni with a snack reception. It was an evening all parents cherished with their children.

As she reached the end of fifth grade, I was proud that she had been determined not only to catch up with her class after her hospital stay but to exceed. Taylor completed great work to move onto sixth grade with her whole class. The Spirt of Excellence award gave Taylor a voice that loudly spoke about who she had become through this whole unexpected ordeal while attending school in the Parkway School District. And this was the start of our journey in finding Superwoman.

Sixth Grade Middle School

Sixth grade had arrived, and so had Taylor. Her new school along with a new system of changing classrooms and walking through halls with older kids, was a little overwhelming at first, but Taylor enjoyed every minute of it. Having attended an open house before school started, I was able to walk the halls with Taylor and complete several run-throughs of classroom routes before school opened. Teachers assured me they would be in the halls until every student reached their class for directions and assured me that the transition would run smoothly, to just give it some time, and not to worry. With a big smile on my face, I said that sounds great.

That year, Taylor had a full academic schedule along with a few elective classes. I wondered how she would balance everything and realized that in time, she would. Her academics went well until I noticed a problem with her math scores. During parent-teachers conferences at her school, the students lead the discussion for their parents. Students had folders with information on each subject, with remarks on each subject. Teachers were standing by to answer questions students could not answer for parents. While flipping through Taylor's folder, I came across her math scores and drew a frown on my face. I asked Taylor what the problem was, and Taylor said she didn't know. I suggested asking her math teacher.

As I approached her math room, I noticed that her teacher had already left. I stopped by the principal's office and spoke to the assistant principal. After a brief conversation about my daughter's math scores, I was told I was not the only parent in that room with concerns about her class. Then, the assistant principal assured me he would speak to the math teacher and figure out the problem.

Meanwhile, I wanted to do something that would help my daughter with her math. We were led to after-school math tutoring. I meet with the math tutor, and she welcomed Taylor into the group. The group grew larger by the week then moved to a larger room where more assistant teachers worked together to help the students.

Before picking up Taylor from afterschool tutoring one evening, I stopped to see if her math teacher was in. A different teacher was there, and we talked about my concerns with Taylor and her math scores. This person soon became my daughter's regular math teacher. The replacement teacher told me that she would be there throughout the rest of the year, and she was monitoring every student due to parental concerns. That meant that I was not the only parent who had approached this new replacement teacher. She noticed that Taylor was using after-school tutoring and thought it was helping a great deal. The replacement teacher did not go into the reason why the original math teacher had left the school so early in the year, but I assumed it was because of all the other complaints about students test scores from parents.

There was no need for the assistant principal to follow up with me on this issue. It looked to me like something was moving in the right direction. And so was Taylor. Her math scores improved, and she was extremely excited. Math tutoring helped Taylor slow down to see the process and ask questions. To see step-by-step problem-solving was a good thing for Taylor. I wondered if Taylor's math scores from the teacher who left so mysteriously were accurate or if Taylor had a problem with the math teacher that she had not talked to me about. Whatever the case might have been, I must say I was pleased and appreciative that the math tutoring helped. It made Taylor more confident about taking tests and enabled her to pass them with higher scores.

As a parent, I wanted to help my daughter with her learning. I tried to help her with her math, but Taylor always came back and said, "No, no, Mom, you're doing it all wrong." Forty years after graduating middle school, I could see math had changed and new methods of learning had been implemented. I just needed to be reassured of this change and my dear daughter was the one to do so. Then, I let the math tutoring teacher take control.

One afternoon, I surprised my daughter and decided to have lunch with her at her school. Taylor was glad to see me, and I was glad to see how well she was handling herself. I wanted to see who Taylor's friends were and how she was surrounding herself with them. Groups, sometimes, made me nervous. And I wanted to make sure Taylor's friends were respectful of her and she was of them. I sat with my daughter and her friends during lunch, and they all were comfortable. I tried to figure out what it meant when one girl said that parents do this kind of stuff, so they got used to it. The group laughed, and I gave a fake smile then left.

I saw what I wanted to see and noticed I was not the only parent doing it. I sat with a positive group that was respectful of each other. I wanted to make sure Taylor was in a healthy environment to learn in the classroom and out. Concerned about bullying and foul language, I needed reassurance my daughter was engaged with a respectful group.

New Tool: Infinte Campus

A new tool for students and parents had arrived: Infinite Campus. I had been waiting for a tool like this one. It allowed students and parents to monitor students' grades and assignments and communicate with teachers and staff members without daily phone calls or face-to-face meetings. Taylor and I were able to use this online tool weekly or daily to check to see if she was on track with her assignments. If grades for assignments were missing, Taylor could send her teacher an email right from the grade book to let her teacher know which assignment it was and that it would be turned in during the next class. Infinite Campus gave me a lot of clarity on my daughter's academics electronically. I was also able to utilize this tool during my lunch period and after work. Taylor could use it during school break, library time, or after school. What a great plus for us. I was able to free up so much time before arriving home so I could spend more family time with my daughter. This was one tool I cherished throughout my daughter's academic years and hoped other parents did the same. It was helpful to us in so many ways. I'm quite sure it was helpful to teachers too.

As the school year wound down, Taylor prepared for her sixth-grade orchestra performance. She was excited to be a part of her middle school orchestra team and excited to showcase her talent. I was also excited to see how much more she had learned in middle school orchestra and how much better she could play her instrument.

Wearing black pants and white shirt, music sheets in order of play, instrument tuned for playing, Taylor was ready for her performance. This was one of their special performances called the All District Orchestra Concert from the Parkway School District. All district middle school's music students were grouped together for a final grand performance. Before the performance, students had one chance to meet for practice together and meet and greet other music students from around the district.

During the start of the performance students were excited to see so many parents in the audience but were also excited to play with so many different middle school students with the same passion as theirs. They came together with grace and poise and played with their hearts on their sleeve with a tune that compliments a year-end concert that was enjoyable to all. The orchestra played, Joseph J. Phillip's "Fantasies on the Original Theme" and John Lennon and Paul McCartney's, "The Beasties Forever." The audience was pleased with the beautiful music.

Taylor had expressed herself well playing the violin, and she too was pleased with her performance. I told her how proud I was of her and smiled as she prepared for bed. She slept soundly that night with joy in her heart. She had expressed herself with a passion for music, and her family and friends saw why she chose the violin. Sixth grade came to an end, and it was a great first year of middle school.

Seventh Grade Middle School

Seventh grade was a good year. Taylor knew how middle school worked, and she knew how to reach her classes before the bell rang. In her orchestra class, Taylor was eager to learn more difficult tunes. She wanted to challenge herself with her music, and I knew she would conquer this task without struggle. It showed just how much she was investing in being a violinist. So, she practiced a lot of challenging music and looked forward to music class.

As she worked hard to stay on top of her academics, there was word that reached parents that some after-school programs would be eliminated that year. To address parental concerns, the school had a meeting with parents to talk about the changes and to answer any question. Sure enough, that very same math tutoring class that has helped my daughter and many other students was disappearing. I spoke to the math tutoring teacher and she confirmed with disappointment.

Taylor and I talked, and she promised me that she would work extra hard on her math to make sure her scores turned out great. She also told me that she would ask more questions in class if she needed help understanding. Nervous but sure of my daughter's promise, I monitored her grades through Infinite Campus almost daily. I felt that if I missed a day of checking her math scores, I just might miss something that I could had helped her with. Turns out that promise my daughter gave me about math turned into a great accomplishment. Losing the math tutoring after-school program gave my daughter confidence that if she worked hard and put more time into her math, she could do well all on her own. Taylor just needed to have more confidence in herself that she could do the work without additional help. Her math tutor gave her that while working together and assured her after math tutoring ended, she would do simply fine. Those words inspired Taylor to believe and trust herself. This progress was also something I was looking for in a school district: one that could give my daughter confidence with her academics.

Seventh grade year came and went with a bang. She had good grades and one big vote of confidence to carry throughout her school year, along with challenging orchestra music to learn. So proud, I was excited that we were on the right track to finding Superwoman. We were looking to be saved from a failing school district. We knew that Superwoman, our hero, would give Taylor the strength, guidance and confidence she needed to continue her academic journey with a great outcome.

Eighth Grade Middle School

Eighth grade was a year of preparation to enter high school at the Parkway School District. Special testing prepared my daughter and other students for high school. The required tests were state mandatory assessment and future ACT/ SAT testing, or both depending on college requirements. Taylor was ready to jump right in. She knew she was just a year away from high school, and she was a little anxious.

We scheduled some mom-and-daughter ice cream social time to talk about it and relax. This was something Taylor and I made sure we did occasionally. Ice cream is an all-time favorite of ours. Relaxing with sweet cream and chatter was always good for us. I asked Taylor to try and enjoy her school years and live them year by year. As I talked to Taylor, I wanted her to know that they go by fast and before she knew it, they would be gone. I wanted Taylor to enjoy the ride and let her academics fall into place and not move too fast. She said she would try as best as possible but knew that task would be hard with more challenging courses to take. Her friends were all talking about high school, and she couldn't wait to experience it for herself. My typical student.

Taylor's academics were looking good. She was preparing to take a test called Aspire. This test helped to show what areas students needed work on before taking the ACT and SAT. Taylor did well and was in the normal range. With several years left before taking her College Entrance Test, Taylor was on the right track but needed more academic leaning from high school to fully prepare her, which is standard procedure for all students before test time.

Road Trip

Taylor was back in music, and things were going great. So great that her orchestra class was invited to Kansas City, Missouri for a competition playoff with surrounding school groups. She was excited because this was her first overnight stay without her mom—plus a road trip with her orchestra group. The orchestra class prepared to do their best and wanted to bring home a trophy. Practicing long hours during school and after, the group put the work in for a great performance.

Surprising themselves, they won first place for their performance and were presented with a trophy for all their hard work. They were also awarded a bonus second performance before leaving. This time at the Worlds of Fun Amusement Park in Kansas City, Missouri. They showcased their skills in front of the amusement park guest. Overjoyed and excited after their performances, the group was ready to have some fun. With lots of rides, fun games, and tons of tasty treats, the kids were off. What a great way to end a road trip.

Wiped out, Taylor was back home from her two-day trip but not too tired to tell me about it. I just listened with joy and smiled with a little sadness. I could see that my daughter was growing up. She was going from not leaving my side unless she was attending school to traveling with fellow students. She handled herself well without me, and it warmed my heart. My daughter was ready to have a little space away from her mom, and I was okay with it.

Middle School Graduation

Accomplishing her very best, Taylor was once again a Spirt of Excellence student while reaching the honor roll. Eighth grade became a breeze for Taylor, and she balanced herself well. Graduation was here, and she was ready for her celebration and to receive her Certificate of Promotion for Completion of Middle School. The graduation program words of wisdom read:

> ***The mission of the***
> ***Parkway School District***
> ***is to ensure all students are***
> ***capable, curious, and confident***
> ***learners who understand and***
> ***respond to the challenges of an***
> ***ever changing world.***

Raising Taylor, Finding Superwoman

I was proud to be Taylor's mom and proud be sitting in the audience to celebrate her accomplishments. Taylor had shown me that she was capable, willing, and ready to meet her high school academic years. As teachers gave their final speeches to their class, the students were overjoyed and ready to say goodbye to middle school. Bursting with joy, the students clapped, yelled, and exclaimed they that they made it through middle school. It was so much fun for them and so much fun to see.

The Difficult Choices Many Parents Find Hard to Make

*Taylor's 4th grade orchestra performance
(1st performance)*

Taylor's All District Concert

Taylor's 1st Spirit of Excellence Award, elementary school (top and below)

The Difficult Choices Many Parents Find Hard to Make

Taylor's Interview for the 2019 Summer Focus Program, St. Louis, Missouri

San Francisco Pier 39 tour

San Francisco Lunch at Fisherman Wharf tour

The Difficult Choices Many Parents Find Hard to Make

San Francisco tall buildings tour

San Francisco cable car

Golden Gate Bridge

The Difficult Choices Many Parents Find Hard to Make

San Francisco Macy's store and tall Christmas tree tour

Raising Taylor, Finding Superwoman

Taylor and Mom, Union Square, San Francisco tour

The Difficult Choices Many Parents Find Hard to Make

Taylor's, 2019 graduation, Parkway North High School

Ninth Grade High School

High school! *Yeah! I'm ready! And I'm here!* So excited to run with the big kids, Taylor was up early. She was ready to go and dragged me with her to the bus stop way earlier than the bus arrival time of 7:05am. Taylor didn't care one bit. She never noticed how long it took the bus to arrive at her stop, which, by the way, was the last pickup before heading to the high school. But rest assured as a parent, I was not too excited about standing at a bus stop early in the morning (before 6:45 am). After seeing Taylor's beautiful smile, I knew then she was relieved and overjoyed she had finally made it to high school. I couldn't help but relax and watch her face shine with a glow from the rising sun. I soon forgot about how early she woke me up to escort her to the bus stop on my day off from work. I watched as she climbed into to the bus and found a seat with a familiar friend. She was comfortable. She was on her own. Mom was not with her to help find classes. Taylor was doing it herself, and she felt good about it.

That year's biggest challenge was balancing her academics with her even more challenging music. Concert 1 Orchestra had more performances than she had before. The music was much more challenging, and she knew all eyes were on them when performing. She would set up her music stand, put her music in order, and tune her violin. Then, she positioned herself as if she were on stage, but she actually was alone in her room. The music started to flow, and she concentrated on hitting the right strings. She knew every practice was important to perform well in front of a large audience.

Preparing for her first performance, Taylor worked hard to make a good first impression. She checked her uniform of black pants which were clean and pressed. Her white shirt was white as snow and ironed to a crisp, put together for a polished look on stage. So proud to be performing in Concert 1 Orchestra, she was ready for the evening. I checked to make sure Taylor was in compliance with her dress code and gave the final approval. We were ready to leave.

As we stepped out the front door, our neighbor's dog decided he wanted to play. He ran and jumped on top of Taylor's very clean black pants and white shirt. As I was yelling to my neighbor to get their dog, it was all too late. White and brown dog hair had rubbed all over Taylor's black pants and paw dirt had landed on her white shirt. I went totally crazy. Ballistic was more like it. Yelling at the dog and the neighbor at the same time with fire in my eyes. I couldn't help but get upset. I calmed down just a little and helped Taylor back into the house to clean her up.

The Difficult Choices Many Parents Find Hard to Make

All of Taylor's high school performances are graded on appearance first as they walked through the door. It was a must that Taylor's outfit was clean and crisp. So, I hurried and found a lint brush and started to brush her black pants from top to bottom. As far as her white shirt went, I dampened a small white towel and briskly rubbed the dirt spots until they looked clean. In the end, the lint brush did a great job with removing the dog hair from her black pants. Her white shirt was a little wet in spots but was clean enough for the performance. My neighbor apologized for the inconvenience, but I was too upset to accept the apology and cracked a fake smile and turned away. We made it to my daughter's performance on time with a cleaned-up uniform, and that was all that mattered to me.

As the Concert 1 Orchestra team was tuning their instruments, Taylor seemed to have forgotten all about the disruption before she arrived. That was a good thing. I wanted Taylor's head to be clear so that she could concentrate on her music and play with passion. This was important. It helped Taylor to become free from distractions, so that she could enjoy the music she was playing. And she did just that. Excited to be playing in Concert 1 Orchestra, Taylor was playing with her heart on her sleeve. She would shift her head and arms to the beat of the music with grace, as did the whole orchestra. They were playing, Lauren Bernofsky, "Wired" to start and then flowing into, Dackow/Vivaldi, "Concerto in G Major" with songs "Presto" and "Allegro," then ending the concert with Elliot Del Borgo's "Dance Infernale." At the end of their performance, the orchestra stood, and the audience was pleased to honor them with a standing ovation. What a beautiful evening of music.

As the school year went by more performances were scheduled, but Taylor didn't mind her full schedule because she had found her passion and loved to be included in a group that shared the same passion as hers. She was balancing academics and orchestra while making good grades. She had once again reached Spirt of Excellence and I was proud of her achievement. She was setting an example for students to come. With hard work, lots of study time, and great concentration, Taylor had a good first year in high school. I honestly believed that music helped Taylor do so well in her academics. She looked forward to playing the violin, and it helped that she had found a passion to express herself. In the end, she was exhausted from her busy school and arts year. As an honor student, Taylor enjoyed every minute of her ninth-grade school year and was excited to move on to tenth grade.

Tenth Grade High School

Back to high school and starting tenth grade, Taylor was all smiles and feeling refreshed from summer break. During summer break, she played golf with the Golf Foundation of Missouri Summer Camp. She did well, better than I thought she would. So well that at the end of summer the golf foundation put together a ceremony, and Taylor was presented with a certificate of participation for her achievement and a brand-new teen golf club set. What a great summer break she had. Fun activities to free her mind from school was what she needed. Learning how to play golf gave her time to relax and enjoy the outdoors and to learn something new. Her instructors were pleased to see how well she concentrated on learning the game. They saw her techniques and dedication to the sport.

Bad Decision: Taking Honors Advanced American History

Taylor received her class schedule, and she understood what was required in her sophomore year of high school. Music was back on the list and so was Honors American History along with all other required academic courses. It was going to be a more demanding year for Taylor, but she was prepared for it-so I thought. Midway through Taylor's first quarter of school, I took the time to look at her grade book closely in Infinite Campus. I noticed that in Honors American History my daughter was behind in her assignments. I asked Taylor, and she said there were too many assignments for her to complete them all on-time. She was working on them and would use her weekend to catch up. By the next week, Taylor was nowhere near completed with all the late assignments, and she had not started working on the new ones. I began to wonder what the problem was. Was Taylor not understanding in this class? Was she not catching on to the material? Was she just behind on doing the assignments or was it because there were too many that was required for Honors American History? Not knowing the answer to these questions, Taylor and I started to brainstorm together to figure out what she needed to do. The first thing was to see her mentor at Parkway High School and ask for help. I told Taylor it was a great suggestion, and I hoped a good plan would be set after their meeting. Well, sorry to say, no luck. Her senior mentor had not taken the course and could not give Taylor much insight on how to keep up.

The Difficult Choices Many Parents Find Hard to Make

She only recommended spending more time working on her Honors American History class assignments but that meant having little time for her other class assignments.

I became worried that at the end of the quarter Taylor would receive a bad grade, so I asked for guidance from Taylor's counselor at her school. Taylor's counselor wanted to speak to the teacher and see if there was anything we could do. Via email from Taylor's teacher, it was suggested that he would take any late assignment and still grade them. He also stated that Taylor was in the right class/course for her skill level. She just needed to coordinate her time and complete the assignments. That would be great, but there was no more time available to catch up before the quarter ended. Taylor's counselor hoped I would change my mind and work with the teacher and not remove her from Honors American History. I just could not see Taylor completing all of her late assignments. I communicated with the counselor to start preparations for Taylor's removal from Honors Advance History. Wanting to salvage the rest of the year I needed to move fast for an available space in Standard American History with the teacher's approval. Taylor tried her best to catch up but, in the end, she just couldn't without falling behind in all of her other classes. It was best for her to be moved to Standard American History for a slower pace. American History was a required course for graduation, and she needed to complete the course with a passing grade. Whether it was Honors American History or Standard American History, we needed a passing grade. The counselor contacted me and wanted me to meet with the teacher to come up with a plan. What I offered was to come to the school for a classroom observation. I wanted to see what was happening in this class and if Taylor was the only student behind. I asked myself why the teacher and counselor were pushing so hard for me not to remove Taylor from this class. I was later declined the visit, and I knew then and recognized that if my daughter was so far behind in her assignments, she would be mentally exhausted to continue to keep up, and it would all fall flat into a wasted year of Honors American History.

As a parent, I felt I was responsible for recognizing any problems that might occur in my daughter's' academic career. I felt that it was my duty as a parent to help her through the process of how to respond to challenges effectively. I never imagined my honor-roll student stressed, exhausted, and unsure about completing one of her courses.

We made the decision together to drop Taylor's Honors American History class and take the standard class, so she could balance all her classes with a great success by the end of the year. And it turned out to be a great choice. Her first semester, she received an F in Honors American History from a ton of late assignments. Second semester in Standard American History, she received an A with on-time assignments. This change proved that parents could help with encouragement in troubled times. I continued to have faith in Taylor to do her best no matter what class she was taking. But I was left with the unanswered question: why did Taylor fall so far behind in Honors American History?

Stress Happens

As the school year continued, I could tell Taylor's stress level was a little high. Working with a full course of academics plus music practice and homework, she was wiped out by bedtime. I spoke to Taylor and encouraged her to hang in there, and that winter break was approaching, and that she would have some much-needed time off soon.

Recognizing Taylor needed something new and relaxing in her life, I planned something exciting for the both of us: a winter vacation. This was the first winter vacation Taylor and I had ever taken. Usually, we took vacations in late spring or summer because of school. But in winter 2017, I knew Taylor needed a reason to get away. So, I planned for us to travel to San Francisco, California, on Christmas Day.

Flying out on Christmas Day was not only exciting, but it was also financially reasonable. We took advantage of all the perks: low airfare and low hotel rates. Excited to leave on our journey, we arrived at the airport early to check in and to have lunch before our flight. Christmas lunch consisted of, burgers and fries, and we didn't mind it, not one bit. We never missed the traditional turkey, ham, and sweet potatoes with pies and cakes. We were excited about getting away and relaxing. The airport was more crowded than I imagined it would be on Christmas Day. But I guessed other travelers had the same ideal as us. We boarded our Southwest flight to San Francisco and the sky was clear, blue, and beautiful. The ride was very pleasant and comfortable.

Once we landed in San Francisco, it felt just like St. Louis, Missouri, with its 40-degree weather. I was disappointed. I had no clue that San Francisco, California, was experiencing cold weather that winter. With a lightweight all-weather jacket on, I was not impressed. My daughter looked at me and started laughing. That was no laughing matter, but it did put a smile on my daughter's face. She found it funny how disappointed I was because of the cold weather, all while I was hoping for fifty or sixty-degree sunny weather. She was now feeling better and relieved that school was out for winter break. For an extra added treat, she was away experiencing her first winter vacation.

We took the airport shuttle to the hotel. No surprise that it was at an outside curb stop where the wind was whipping around my face. The shuttle arrived, and Taylor and I hopped in for the ride. As we arrived at the hotel, we checked-in and asked the beautiful hostess for a good place to eat. The hostess smiled and said that their restaurant was closed for the Christmas holiday, but we could choose from Chinese food or pizza. Tasty! She assured me that they were open this Christmas Day with business flowing in and out. Before I could open my mouth, I had forgotten that we were traveling on Christmas Day and many restaurants were closed to observe the holiday. Taylor and I took what we could get. We chose pizza for dinner Christmas Night.

The pizza place was busy. Lots of people were dinning out that night and not having the traditional Christmas leftovers. We stood in line and waited our turn and ordered to go because

The Difficult Choices Many Parents Find Hard to Make

all seats were taken. Once we got back to the hotel, we ate dinner and soon drifted off to bed.

The next morning, the restaurant was open and ready for business. Taylor and I had a full breakfast and began our journey. First up, all-day shopping at Union Square. What a San Francisco treat! The weather was warmer, so we were able to walk, sightsee, and shop. We started at the top of Union Square and made our way down to the bottom. Smart move, because San Francisco has the steepest hills I had every come across. We noticed that the line for the cable car was long as we journeyed down to the end and found out why as we struggled to walk back up to the top.

Out of breath and making up excuses to stop several times, I asked Taylor if she wanted some lunch. She replied yes. Stop one. "Taylor, would you like some desert?" She replied yes. Stop two. "Taylor, would you like to see the choir sing Christmas carols?" And of course, she replied yes again. The Christmas carols performance was right in front of San Francisco's big Macy's store surrounded by a very tall, decorated Christmas tree. Sitting and enjoying the season's music we felt like we were in the movie *A Christmas Story*. Children's singing, laughing, running, and jumping with joy; parents drinking coffee or hot chocolate; this seasonal event was enjoyable. This was stop three, which was our last stop to the top of the hill.

We waited for the shuttle bus to return to Union Square for pickup, and I was smiling because we made it back up San Francisco's steep hills. By stopping several times for breaks along the way, I had time to rest and experience additional sights. Taylor told me later that she knew I needed to stop a few times because I was out of breath and said she enjoyed every resting place and didn't mind. I thought that was great because I surely could not climb another hill without the stoppage.

The next morning, we were prepared to sightsee the whole day. Starting with lunch at Fisherman's Wharf of San Francisco, we had the best fish and chips in town with a small bowl of seafood soup while enjoying the sights of Pier 39. We then took the Big Bus Tours of San Francisco. Sitting on the top deck of the tour bus, we enjoyed many views of tall buildings like pyramids. We enjoyed seeing the vintage-style homes, the Embarcadero Center, and San Francisco Cathedral. We also enjoyed seeing many cable cars go by full of passengers hanging on the outer rails rolling up and down steep hills. We experienced a great deal of San Francisco's steep hills, but this time without walking. The bus was full of people from all states and the driver handled the hills with experience and care. It felt like we were on a roller coaster ride reaching the top slowly then topping it off with a fast ride downhill. The passengers seemed to enjoy the ride above and below deck with so much fun.

Traveling through the city we made it to our last stop. This stop is what we had been waiting for all day: The Golden Gate Bridge. This was one of the best and most popular attractions in San Francisco. People from all over were thrilled to see it, walk across it if possible, and experience the beautiful view. As we approached the bridge, while riding the top of the bus, we were able to take some great pictures from above. When we arrived at the end of the bridge, we exited the bus quickly to experience the late evening walk across the Golden Gate Bridge. With nightfall approaching, the wind was behind us. It was cold and bitter, but the beautiful bridge was lighted to direct our steps. Taylor and I enjoyed the walk and scenery through it all.

As we headed back to the bus we climbed aboard and were told the only seats left were on top. And then a "oh no" look appeared on our faces. It was fun to ride the top of the bus during the afternoon hours with lots of sun, but the late evening to night hours were torture. Wind and cold created one unpleasant ride. Up and down steep hills, the growling wind attacked us from left to right and back to front. Ugh! What a horrible ride back to the hotel. Happy to get back, Taylor and I turned up the heat like it was below zero. We could not get warm fast enough. But in the end, we laughed and talked about what we experienced. We enjoyed our tour of San Francisco and the walk across the Golden Gate Bridge. What a sight and a great feeling to experience with one of the most popular tourist sites in San Francisco.

We had one more day of excitement before we headed home. I planned to take Taylor to see the Golden State Warriors basketball team. Before the game, Taylor and I had a mother and daughter lunch to spend some quality time together to see how she was feeling. She said she was happy we took the trip and loved the activities we had experienced so far. We talked about the game and what she was expecting. Lots of people, loud noise, DJ spinning music, good treats, and, of course, to see her favorite basketball player, Stephen Curry in person. Taylor was so excited she just burst with a big smile of joy.

After lunch, we headed out to the Oracle Arena to experience it all. Just a great evening for us and for the Golden State Warriors. They played Toronto and won the game. Allstar players were there and on the court for warm-up. They all played several minutes of the game. We were happy to see them. Sometimes, parents spend countless dollars to take their kids to NBA games which require travel, hotel lodging, food, and other necessities a family may need during their trip—not to mention seating tickets to enter the arena. After spending so much money to attend NBA games, you hope your favorite players are there and playing in the game. It's disappointing when you find out your favorite player is off for the evening or has sustained injuries and cannot play. But we understand injuries do happen and may not be preventable. It's still disappointing when you spend so much money to support your favorite team and your favorite players are not there playing. I think kids take it the hardest because they get excited when they see a role model, or a favorite celebrity and they expect them to be there. This time Taylor and I hit the jackpot. We bought tickets, we experienced the excitement and saw the Golden State Warriors Team live and in action. Well worth the dollars spent to enjoy an exciting evening with the Warriors.

Time to say goodbye. Taylor and I were up early the next morning to have our final breakfast in San Francisco before heading home. We enjoyed our trip from start to finish. We experienced great relaxing events with beautiful tour sites. Our first winter vacation was a true hit. I was so glad I recognized the need for my daughter to get away. I was relieved that Taylor was able to find this outlet to relieve her stress from school. We would not take a trip like this every year, but I promised that we would do something relaxing to help my daughter when stress occurs during her academic years. Heading home but sad to leave, we vowed to return to enjoy more of San Francisco. There was so much more to see, but time was short and sweet, and we had to go. But next time it would be in the spring or early fall hoping to avoid another cold winter spell and our stay would be a little longer.

Refreshed

Back in St. Louis, Missouri, we were renewed. Taylor was ready for the second semester of school, and we were looking forward to her sweet sixteen birthday. Although Taylor just had a great winter vacation, I planned something small and surprising for her birthday. I recruited one of Taylor's friends to gather a small group after their Orchestra Concert 2 performance. Not giving a hint what was going on, I asked Taylor to return to the gym after storing her instrument in the orchestra room after performance time. By that time, a few of her friends were in the gym lined in a half circle to sing

"Happy Birthday" to Taylor and to place a sixteen sash across her shoulders. This sash had "Sweet Sixteen" written across it like the "Miss America" sash worn in the pageant. It was black with white letter's in italics, flowing down her right side with a bow to tie on the hip. It looked beautiful with Taylor's black pants and crisp white shirt from her performance.

After the song, I then brought out delicious, beautiful cupcakes from the CUP! This was one of Taylor's favorite cupcake shops. The girls each took a cupcake and stood around like a football tailgate party, eating cupcakes, laughing, and talking about their performance and sixteenth birthdays. That year, all of her friends turned sixteen, so they had so much to share about the experience.

They shared great moments together with Taylor and wished her well on her sixteenth birthday. We all said our goodbyes for the evening. Taylor looked at me and said, "Thanks, Mom. I was surprised. I didn't think you were going to do anything for my birthday because we just took a great trip." I smiled and told Taylor that sixteen is a special year and I wanted to do something to surprise her. Big or small, I wanted to do something. She hugged me and thanked me for thinking of her and her friends.

Things were moving along swiftly with Taylor's academics. Year end was approaching, and Taylor wanted to finish strong. Final exams were on the table, and Taylor was working hard to prepare for her tests. Feeling a little nervous, Taylor studied for two final exams at a time to pace herself from getting stressed.

All together she had a total of six or seven exams with no more than three tests scheduled in a day. This flexible schedule allowed students to plan their final exam study time day by day. After finals were over, Taylor was once again relieved. She smiled, knowing that she has made Spirts of Excellence and excited to be an honor roll student. We were pleased with her achievement. Then she made a list of fun things to do for the summer.

Not So Fast: Summer School

Remember that first-ever grade F Taylor received in Honors Advanced American History? She now had to complete the first semester over for a passing grade. Feeling okay about it, Taylor signed up for summer school to complete this task. As Taylor walked into Standard American History class for the summer, she noticed more familiar faces from her honors course. Taylor didn't ask why they were there. She just thought maybe Honors American History didn't work out as planned with them over the course of the year as well. Smiling, she took a seat and began to work through the first semester of Standard History for a good grade. She wasn't ashamed to be there. She just wanted a good passing grade. This was Taylor's first time ever taking summer classes. As her academic years went by, she found that taking more courses in the summer and having a head start for her fall schedule was not a bad idea. She breezed through summer school with another A for Standard American History to replace her bad grade in

Honors American History. Our hero has arrived. Looks like Superwoman saved the day once again.

I must say this had been a challenging year for Taylor, although she handled it well. She made good decisions and some bad decisions. But in the end, they all turned out great. Another year bites the dust, and Taylor was moving on to her junior year of high school.

Eleventh Grade High School

Hard Decision

Taylor made the decision not to join the orchestra team this year, and what a smart move it was. Her academics has picked upped considerably for her junior year of high school. She was preparing for college courses and important tests like the ACT, US Constitution, Missouri Assessment, and the Missouri Government and Constitution test. With her demanding schedule, along with all these important tests, Taylor knew she needed more time to prepare. So, she was foregoing orchestra that year, and Mom supported her decision. It was always a joy to hear and see Taylor perform, but with my demanding career in aerospace it was a relief to have a little time for myself and not have to schedule in Taylor performances.

As Taylor's junior year of high school progressed, I received an invitation for Taylor to apply for a summer position at Washington University in St. Louis, Missouri. I spoke to Taylor about the position and her face lit up into a beautiful glow. The position required her to do medical research and give an end-of-the-summer presentation from the focus program. Taylor was excited to hear about the position and about the challenge. Doing quite well in science, biology, and chemistry in high school, Taylor enjoyed the research part. She also enjoyed working in a group setting with other students. The name of the program was the Young Scientists Summer Focus Program at Washington University School of Medicine at the St. Louis, Missouri Campus.

I knew the university was rigorous, so the application was going to be long and the process would take a while. This meant we needed to start early to ensure all requirements were met. On the application, there were more than several questions to ponder along with requests for recommendation letters from her current and past teachers. She needed official transcripts from her school and to complete an essay. I mentioned to Taylor that we needed to jump right on the request because her teachers and counselors were busy with their regular work schedules and her request along with other student requests might be a little overwhelming to complete in a small period of time. So, we got busy. We received all her recommendation letters and attached them to her application along with her electronic transcripts and her beautifully crafted essay. Then finally, right before the deadline, Taylor's application was complete and sent. With a long sigh of relief, we prayed and tried to move on to the next task without thinking about the outcome.

A few weeks after, The YSP reviewed all applications. Taylor was one chosen candidate who received an invitation for a face-to-face interview. Excited about the news, we realized Taylor was going to her very first interview at one of the most highly recognized universities. Washington University in St. Louis, Missouri is a top university that students from all over strive to be accepted into. Taylor knew it would be a great honor and pleasure to be part of this Summer Focus Team with the university or any program at Washington University for that matter. She also knew it would boost her academic résumé. So, Taylor accepted the interview with great joy. With a wide smile on her face, she arrived at the Young Summer Program department an hour ahead of her interview time. That gave Taylor time to relax and soak up the moment. She admired the Washington University Medical Building. It was brick inside and out with lots of inspiring artwork and encouraging letters of wisdom posted on the walls. This building showed and helped build confidence that all things are possible. Taylor was told in an introduction meeting that she would be interviewed by three different groups. She would move from room to room and answer questions from various leaders from the program. Extremely excited, Taylor said she was ready for the interview.

I was nervous for Taylor and could not sit still. I walked the halls of Washington University Medical School trying to stay calm, but the excitement was just too overwhelming. Seeing the wonderful artwork and statues that were posted throughout the university brought me great pleasure. I noticed that the university presented a path of encouragement and achievement for its students. The artwork and statues gave students visual insight from positive thinkers. This reminded me of an award that I received from a distributor company years ago while working to reach my next goal. The award reads:

ATTITUDE

A positive thinker sees the invisible, feels the intangible and achieves the impossible.

By Successors Life Scrape Lithographs

What a statement this award has made. Not only to me, but now I have passed it along to another positive thinker. And hope Taylor will always remember this lesson and carry it with her throughout her journey as I have.

Reflecting back as a positive thinker, I remember bringing Taylor on this very same campus at seven months old. We had a family friend visiting from the Caribbean, and he wanted to tour the university as a study-abroad student. He wanted to find out more information about different programs to see if it was possible for him to apply for admission. Taylor was small and active with burst of cries, so I waited patiently in the halls for our family friend. I tried to keep Taylor occupied by showing her the brick walls and the vivid pictures around the university. I was trying desperately to help her focus on something just to keep her quiet. Well, it worked for a while but then her crying returned. Soon after, our family friend had

The Difficult Choices Many Parents Find Hard to Make

returned with the information he was seeking. We said our goodbyes to the administrator and toured other sites of the city. I had no idea that after bringing Taylor to this campus at seven months old that she would return many years later for her very own interview. I whispered in her ear several times while we were there that she would return someone day. And on March 10, 2018, she had.

Overjoyed, and excited by happy memories we returned to a place where it all started. Taylor at seven months old was a moment to remember at the university. After gathering my composure, I returned to the area where Taylor's interview had been held. I sat down and waited calmly until she finished. Then, when I saw her, I was sure she had done a good job. So excited, I asked Taylor if she would like some lunch and to talk about how the interview went. We headed out to a nearby restaurant and ordered. We sat down, and I looked at Taylor to see if I could make out any expressions that could tell me how she did. She showed little emotions. That was because she was teasing me.

Then it just came out I asked, "Taylor, how did things go?"

She smiled and replied, "It went well, I think."

I asked, "Were there any questions that you could not answer?"

She said, "They told me at first that it was okay if I could not answer all questions. They wanted to get to know me as a person and how I would interact with other students in the program."

I then asked, "Were you asked any questions that you could have answered differently after the interview ended?"

She said, "No, I think I did a good job at my interview."

So proud of my daughter, a big smile appeared on my face. Taylor handled her first interview well with calmness and great composure. I was overjoyed that Taylor was taking charge of her academic journey and choosing programs that would benefit her and challenge her at the same time. Taylor and I discussed that it was a good time to thank the group of team leaders who interviewed her with a letter.

Her thank you letter reads:

The Difficult Choices Many Parents Find Hard to Make

Washington University,
Young Scientist Program, Summer Focus

Thank you, letter,

Taylor

March 13, 2018

Director YSP Summer Focus
Washington University

Dear Director,

It was a pleasure speaking to you and your interview team last Saturday regarding a summer position with The Young Scientist Program at Washington University. I appreciate the time you and your team took out of your schedules to interview me. The whole team made me comfortable and appreciative. I am excited about the opportunity to join a group of rising star students and to work with a great group of professional leaders as yourself and the YSP team. I find the program to be rewarding and rich in learning and helpful to me in furthering my education with exciting new challenges.

If you have any more questions that I may answer, please feel free to contact me. I look forward to hearing from you and The Young Scientist Program team. Thanking you once again.

Sincerely,

Taylor

Now We Wait

It had been a few weeks since Taylor's interview, and we waited patiently for the results. I guess I can say the nervous part had disappeared, and the anxious part had appeared. We wanted to know the outcome and would accept whatever the decision may be. Accepted or not, Taylor achieved a goal and conquered her fears. She applied at a highly recognized university and out of hundreds of applications she was one of the select few to receive an invitation for an interview. She handled herself with great pride and poise.

Preparing Ourselves

Time to move on. Taylor and I had talked, and we both agreed that it would be a good idea to apply for another college summer program. We looked into Maryville University, and their program was a short two-week college prep course, but it would give Taylor some experience before she started her next journey. So, we applied, and Taylor was accepted. What a relief this took off our minds. While we waited on Washington University's response, it became tougher each day we didn't hear from them. Maryville University's project was just what we needed. Something else to pursue while we waited.

Sad News But Not Disappointing

Washington University of St. Louis, Missouri responded. Here is what they said:

The Difficult Choices Many Parents Find Hard to Make

It has been a great pleasure meeting you and interviewing you for our Summer Focus Program. It saddens me to bring the news that you are not a chosen candidate for the program. We wish you good luck on your journey for a great summer program to help you succeed.

Not the news Taylor and I was expecting, but it was also not too sad and disappointing. Taylor received a final face-to-face interview from a great university. She beat out hundreds of applicants all over the metro area that had applied for the summer focus program and who did not receive an interview. Taylor was up against some of the sharpest and smartest students from various high schools in the area. Only fifteen rising stars were accepted. Knowing this, Taylor was excited that she received an opportunity to showcase her academics to a prestigious university. She did so with honor. This was why we were not totally disappointed. We accepted their decision that Taylor was not chosen to be part of their program and understood that the current years talent pool of applicants was so great that the decision must have been hard and stressful with choosing the best participate. This process taught Taylor how to prepare for her next opportunity.

Ending Junior Year

Taylor was all set to attend Maryville University. She has decided to give herself some rest time before starting. That meant Taylor would relax part of her summer vacation and regroup before heading to her college summer program. She had just finished another great school year and deserved the time off. Not to say it was a little tense and stressful, but she made it through.

She then received another invitation for an honors evening before ending her school year. She accepted her administrator award which recognized her outstanding academics grades along with another Spirt of Excellence Award. We were excited that she had the strength and inspiration to focus on her studies while searching for college summer programs. This program would help her pursue and prepare her for early admission to college. Plus, her dual credit helped Taylor to bypass her college algebra course and cruise into college precalculus.

That year was exciting with Taylor's drive and focus to succeed. She put the work in for a great outcome. She has passed the test of focus. She has pushed herself to learn more and to finish strong. She was looking forward to some rest time but was also excited about attending a university to further her academic journey.

INTRODUCING SENIOR YEAR

Twelfth Grade High School

Taylor had arrived. I was smiling because Taylor could see clearly now and she could enjoy her last year of high school as a confident senior. I was excited because I knew our hero Superwoman was within reach. There we were, finally, and the excitement began. But senior year didn't hit Taylor just yet, only me. It seemed like another year of school to her. This was unbelievable that my kid was not excited to be a senior. Not jumping for joy. Just another routine school year for Taylor.

That year was what I called the "Test Year." So many tests were taken to prepare for college. I filled my calendar and to-do-list with all of Taylor's reminders and mines too. I was going crazy keeping it all together. Our calendar was overflowing, and it was challenging to make sure everything got done.

I saw how things had changed since I was a senior back in 1985. It was so simple then. You signed up to take the

ACT test, send scores to your choice of college, received the acceptance letter, took a tour, meet your counselor, filled out your schedule, paid for classes, then showed up for class. It was so simple thirty-five years ago. The process has definitely changed over the decades. Students today start by taking many tests to see where they are academically along with academic counseling and résumé writing. Then the process continued with applying for scholarships, completing college applications with requirements, visit/tour colleges, research programs with financial planning, and the list keeps getting bigger and bigger. This challenge was not only stressful for students but for parents as well.

As we started to look for choice colleges, we were greeted with requirements. Yes, requirements that must be met in order to have a chance of being accepted into their school. I was blown away, but Taylor was calm, very calm for some reason. *Like it's no big deal, Mom! I got this! Chill please! Okay, Daughter, I'm chilled! But I was starting to worry.*

We recorded the requirements and started at the top to make sure we checked them off before we began to fill out the applications. Mostly all colleges required the ACT test, and some accepted the SAT test or both with an essay or without an essay, depending on your college requirements. Taylor was weighing her options on which test was best and whether she should take them both. I suggested that she concentrate on one test and do as well as possible, so she would not overextend herself and stress herself out trying to master them both. After making a final decision to take the ACT test, Taylor realized her first ACT test scores were a little low. I then suggested that she take it again halfway through her senior year because she still had high school precalculus math and some elective English to finish up. Smart move. Her last few months of learning helped her to do better on her second attempt at the ACT Test.

Moving down the list of requirements, we found that with her early childhood learning and academic teaching throughout the years, Taylor was all set to go. Early childhood learning gave Taylor passion to be present every day in a classroom setting with other students. They learned the basic numbers, letters, speaking, singing, and writing techniques at an early age. She loved every bit of her childhood learning years. I enrolled Taylor in a learning daycare at the age of one so that she could start leaning early and be prepared for kindergarten and first grade. She was present almost every day to learn which gave her a passion for belonging to a group and learning together in a group setting.

The next requirement listed was to have a great GPA average, and Taylor has met this one with an above GPA of 3.6. Following that requirement students needed to have a good attendance record. Taylor has kept her attendance above 98 percent yearly with her love and passion to attend school, so this was also met. And the last requirement was to show and state something that stands out about students during their high school years. Taylor has various things that stood out. Her interview at Washington University Focus Group. Her candidacy for Seal of Biliteracy for secondary language, as she is proficient in speaking French and her Spirt of Excellence achievement throughout her secondary school years with being an honor-roll student. And let's not forget years of Orchestra and Concert 1, & 2 performances. Our last and final request was to required documents for supporting material to be sent with her college application. Résumé, transcripts, recommendation letters, honor awards—all had to be verified for her college application. Time for a *long* sigh of relief because this has been one huge task. It took weeks to gather this information for verification. We knew this so we went step by step until all areas were complete.

Audit Time

Meanwhile it was time to check Taylor's senior academic audit for graduation. I received it electronically and reviewed it, then I forward it to Taylor. We noticed a small error that Taylor had not taken the U.S. Government Test, which is a required test for graduation. I asked Taylor, and she was sure that in her junior year she completed the course and passed the test. I double-checked her grades from last year, and it stated just that. I then sent an email to her graduation counselor. At the beginning of each calendar school year, an academic counselor was chosen to oversee all graduates. Their duties were to check grades and required classes with passing state tests to make sure students have enough credits for graduation. If the graduating counselor saw a problem, they would then send out an audit review form to teachers, students, and parents to address. This allowed time for each student who needed additional credits to graduate to take them before their graduation ceremony.

I received a fast response that there was an error with some students test scores. Somehow the U.S. Government test scores from Taylor's class were not uploaded and recorded into the system. I was then told via email that the error was being corrected and handled. This was one reason why it was so important that students, and parents, check their senior academic audit list early in the year because errors do occur, and mistakes do happen. No student should find out at the last minute that an error has occurred on their graduation audit to prevent or delay the student from graduating. And a second pair of eyes with questions were always good to make sure students were on the right path to graduation.

I was very appreciative that Taylor's graduation counselor sent me the audit and that they were aware of the error. But I pondered one question: if they knew about the error, why not alert the effected students and parents before the audits were sent out. That would have avoided questions that would overwhelm the graduation school counselor. I was trying to keep the peace and not ask too many questions. But I did get the feeling that things were getting a little tense, and I did not want to add more smoke to the grill. I felt that I was not the only parent who caught this error on the audit and the emails and phone calls started to become overwhelming for the counselor. About four months later, we received an official audit form that the error was corrected. Taylor was safe for graduation and had started to prepare for her month-long celebration in May 2019. What a relief.

Prom night, high school senior walk, senior picnic, candlelight ceremony, graduation practice, graduation ceremony and graduation bash with a family dinner celebration. Sounds exhausting, but I kept telling Taylor she only gets to do this once in a lifetime and to enjoy it. After high school graduation, she wouldn't have the chance to go back to celebrate, so I wanted Taylor to participate and enjoy every moment of her senior celebration.

Growing Up

I looked at Taylor and saw how much she had changed over the years. Growing from a little girl just starting out to now becoming a young lady. She was confident and positive about her future and was very academically driven. She had been molded into a beautiful young lady. She was not the little girl from years ago who loved Dora the Explorer and the Wimpy Kid Diaries. She grew brighter, smarter and had become her own person right before my eyes. She had her eyes set on achievement and was focused on how to balance her workload. This was one amazing view. I could have not seen it seventeen years ago, but I must say I was pleasantly surprised at how well-groomed she had become.

Honor Programs

Seal of Biliteracy Program

Before ending her senior year, Taylor received an invitation to apply for the Seal of Biliteracy Program. This program required each candidate to take a second language test and to complete a project for the Seal of Biliteracy. If all went well, Taylor would be honored with a seal on her diploma for proficiency in French, her second language. Seven dedicated years of French would pay off with a smile and a seal on her diploma if she completed all testing with a passing score. Taylor and I were overjoyed that she was chosen and felt honored and excited to be a part of the program.

Having a lower score to be accepted in the program, Taylor was just shy of meeting Seal of Biliteracy requirements. We were not disappointed because it is a great joy to learn a second language and to be able to share that language with people who speak it. Taylor's hard work over the years learning French would continue to be an asset to her résumé as a proficient second language speaker.

Spirt of Excellence

Taylor's senior honor award program began on April 16, 2019. She accepted her senior year Spirt of Excellence Award on this date. Being in the program over the past seven years, Taylor had maintained her academic grade point average above 3.5 cumulative. She prioritized her academics first on her list to achieve this great award. We were thankful and honored she received it over the years. She looked to be a great role model for other future students who were trying to do the same.

Another honor ceremony was at the end of the academic school year in May 2019 at her high school. All selected students were invited, and seniors were overjoyed that their journey was about to end with honors. Taylor was excited as well and ready to accept her administrator awards and along with an academic award showing her dedication over the years. I was so proud to be sitting in the audience to cheer my daughter on with all the other parents.

As the school year ended, it was getting close to Taylor's final destination. The high school had a candlelight ceremony for graduating students. The ceremony was a reflection over the senior year as seniors revisited homecoming football events like their homecoming dance and special activities from the year such as assembles, bake sales, music performances, and sports events with volunteer assignments. A video was presented with highlights from these events to spotlight the school's special moments.

The evening then tops off with a special lighting of candles. Some parents were afraid students would drop their lighted candle on the protective vinyl covering on the gym floor due to all the excitement. But we held our breaths and with a long sigh of relief at the end it did not happen. All good and seniors were ready to blow out the light to end their high school journey. What a special night for all graduating seniors.

Graduation

Finding Superwoman

During Taylor's graduation, I realized that we finally found Superwoman. Over the course of Taylor academic years in the Parkway School District, we obtained just what she needed: encouragement, inspiration, a challenging and rewarding academics, along with an accredited school district. Tears of joy poured from my eyes as I wept with a smile on my face. I knew our journey had been with ups and downs, joys and disappointments, gives and takes. We changed various school districts in order to find a district that would be the right fit for Taylor. We needed great academics, along with communication and arts, that could inspire, encourage and challenge her to do her very best and achieve her highest goals. This was when I was sure I had found our hero, Superwoman. Taylor's journey had now come to an end, and she too knew that we made the right choice with choosing the Parkway School District.

Before leaving for Taylor's graduation ceremony, I asked Taylor to take some time in a private setting and look into the mirror and say, "I am beautiful. I am capable and confident. I can accomplish my dreams. I just finished twelve years of school in a challenging school district with great academics. If I can accomplish these things, others can too."

My reason for asking Taylor to recite these lines was for her to hear her encouraging words and her accomplishments.

I wanted her to feel the moment of completion in accepting her high school diploma with Cum Laude Honors.

As her mom, I saw that Taylor needed more from me A mom who did more than tell her to go to school and do her homework while raising her. She needed a mom who could recognize her needs throughout her childhood academic years. She needed a mom to give her good guidance on how to find her way through school and how to contribute to her school. With the help of her mom, we found Superwoman our way. We invested in the Parkway School District and accepted their invitation for them to invest in my daughter's academics as well.

Finding Superwoman Our Way

I'm telling our story to share our accomplishments, knowing that someone else is also trying to find Superwoman. I'm using my voice to let people know they are not alone. I want people to know that we had good choices and bad choices with options to choose and uncertain times. Knowing that some choices came with challenges to overcome. We had to give up our home, community, and friends close by in order to achieve our goals, and that is the very hard decision some parents have to make. It wasn't easy going through twelve years of uncertainty. But knowing that I made the best decision for Taylor and believing with great faith that things will turn out well, gave me the assurance I needed to continue the path we chose. I knew in my heart that what was taken away would return to us. And that was all I needed while raising Taylor to start her academic journey in Finding Superwoman. There is a reason why Superwoman is our hero. Because *heroes accomplish great things*. And so did Taylor!

Understanding Both Sides of the Aisle

Recently I found out that Riverview School Garden District (Taylor's first school district) just received their accreditation back after a long decade of working without it. I congratulate the school district on achieving this goal. No parent, mentor, student, or teacher wants to lose faith in a school district that has failed the community. Riverview Gardens brought this faith back to the community. They have shown that students should and could receive a good education within their community. I commend them on the great work they have put forth over the years to regain their accreditation. But when a school district loses their accreditation, parents have choices and options to decide what is best for their children and their family.

Parents wants more from a school district for their child's education. Parents are looking for great academics with a continuous improvement plan to show that the school district wants to achieve more with its students in all areas. Parents look for good standards in teaching and testing to help their children throughout their academic years. And that was why I made my decision to move my daughter. I needed all these things and more for her.

Taylor and I made the decision to move to another district because I never received a firm answer on when and how the school district would regain its accreditation. That was unsettling to me. We made this choice to move to a challenging school district that could give Taylor what she needed in all areas to succeed, and we never looked back. Turns out that was the best choice for us because we could not wait a decade for Riverview Garden School District to turn their academics around and to reinstate their accreditation.

So this is why I understand both sides of the aisle. School districts want to keep all students in their community to teach them and give them the good education they deserve, but parents want more and make hard decisions to move their children to a better school district when their community school's district accreditation has been lost. I looked for a school that had great academics with college—readiness programs and one with an accreditation seal of approval.

But for me as a parent, I realized I had choices and chose the best option for my daughter, which lead me to another school district that could offer the things my daughter needed to complete her first twelve years of school with honors. I'm overjoyed we made the right decision for us. Years of living with neighbors who we grew to care for, with a community where we both felt safe, disappeared. We left with uncertainty but with faith on our side, unsure of each year that flew by Taylor worked hard to assure me that things would turn out great. Did I question our decision to move? Yes, I did. Many times. But I became comfortable moving forward without looking back. That is the very tough part about choices when it comes to your child's education. Not all households can make the decision we made, but all parents have choices and options that they can ponder into making the decision that best fits their children's educational and family needs.

Conclusion

I never gave up hope that Taylor would achieve her best. I always supported her. In good times and bad. No matter what the outcome was or how long it took her to reach her goals, I was always positive. Even when people doubted her ability, I did not. In my eyes, a parent's support gives children faith and hope that helps them dream of reaching their goals and accomplishing them. I did just that, and the outcome was greater than I ever imagined.

As her mother, I felt I failed at Taylor's education in the beginning. I blamed myself for not recognizing the loss of a troubled community school district. I blamed myself for not having my eyes on my daughter's education prior to enrolling her in school, even knowing that the school district was the one who failed us. Riverview Garden School District failed us before we could get off to a good start. As a parent, you want the best for your child and to give them everything possible, they need to succeed. It hurts when parents have difficult decisions to make because of a failing school district.

But when you realize that you must make some hard choices in order to help them accomplish their goals, you feel the weight on your shoulders. This was when I realized I had options. I told myself I can choose the best educational path for my daughter. That this decision was mine to make and not the school district. I made this decision due to a failing school district that had no idea when they would regain their accreditation.

I truly believe that it was my responsibility to help my daughter succeed with great teaching and learning in school and out. But in the end, I needed the school district that failed us to accept some of the responsibility. I moved my daughter to a better school district that could give her what she needed and could continue to improve for all students who followed. And what a great choice it turned out to be. But a difficult one for us and the community we both loved so much.

Who Is This Book For?

This book is for parents, guardians, mentors, teachers, principals, counselors, communities, and curious readers. It is for your reading enjoyment and not to follow our path. This is our story, and I am using my voice to share it. Its written to let some readers know I have been where you are and that you are not alone. This book is to help readers to see, that there's always hope, always options and always choices to make. We all have difficult choices to make in our lifetime and we all believe that things will turn out well. This book is my expression of how I raised Taylor throughout her academic school years and how we managed to find *Superwoman our way.* I'm sharing our story because I think it's important to others, who like me, thought there was no path to finding a great educational system for my daughter while living in a failed school district. But with the help from resources, counselors, and my own research I was able to make some tough decisions. Feeling assured that I made the right decision I knew that everything we gave up will return to us. I'm using my voice as a tool to share our story and the accomplishments gained throughout our journey. **Finding Superwoman Our Way!**

Taylor's Update College Year One

Today, Taylor is doing great. Not only has she regained her balance back, but she has also found a passion for therapy. I am pleased to say Taylor has been accepted into University of Central Florida and the University of South Florida, Tampa Bay. Her hard work paid off. Her academics met both school requirements for acceptance into these great universities. We are pleased to announce that she accepted University of Central Florida as her college choice. This college is not only a good academic college, but it also focuses on family, too. We love the family feeling as we attend college football games and various family events on campus. The whole family is always welcome. Taylor is enrolled in the STEM program seeking a biology undergraduate degree then moving on to graduate school to become an occupational therapist.

Besides attending a great University, Taylor is at one of the happiest places on earth. Central Florida brings her the relaxation from the beach with a great saltwater smell. She also enjoys spending time at Disney World and shopping at Disney Springs to release her stress from college time to time. As we all know, Walt Disney World is a dream place of its own. It helps people to imagine themselves reaching their goals. Taylor feels she made the right choice and feels free and liberated to be in Central Florida attending one of their great university in Florida.

www.ingramcontent.com/pod-product-compliance
Lightning Source LLC
Chambersburg PA
CBHW072224200426
43209CB00073B/1929/J